IN A TIME OF VIOLENCE

# In a Time of Violence

## EAVAN BOLAND

W. W. NORTON & COMPANY
NEW YORK / LONDON

. . . . . .

The text of this book is composed in Centauer.
Composition by PennSet, Inc.
Manufacturing by The Courier Companies, Inc.

BOOK DESIGN BY CHRIS WELCH.

Library of Congress Cataloging-in-Publication Data
Boland, Eavan.
    In a time of violence / by Eavan Boland.
        p.   cm.
    Poetry.
    I. Title.
    PR6052.O35I49    1994
    821'.914—dc20                          93-32371

ISBN 0-393-03617-0

W. W. Norton & Company, Inc.
500 Fifth Avenue,
New York, N.Y. 10110
W. W. Norton & Company Ltd.
10 Coptic Street,
London WC1A 1PU

1   2   3   4   5   6   7   8   9   0

# Contents

## III / Anna Liffey

# Acknowledgements

Acknowledgements are made to the editors of the following publications in which some of these poems appeared, sometimes in a different form and with different titles.
*The New Yorker* "The Pomegranate"; "The Dolls Museum in Dublin"; "A Sparrow Hawk in the Suburbs"; "Love"; "The Water Clock" · *The Paris Review* "Inscriptions"; "At The Glass Factory in Cavan Town" · *American Poetry Review* "Anna Liffey" · *The Atlantic* "The Death of Reason" · *The Partisan Review* "In a Bad Light" · *The Kenyon Review* "What Language Did" · *The Seneca Review* "We Are the Only Animals Who Do This" · *The Yale Review* "A Woman Painted on a Leaf" · *The New Republic* "The Parcel" · *Poetry* "In Which the Ancient History I Learn Is Not My Own" · *PN Review and Poetry Ireland* "At The Glass Factory in Cavan Town" · "Inscriptions" was included in the Pushcart Prize volume of 1992 and was published in *The Poetry Book Society Anthology 1991* · "Lava Cameo" was awarded the Daniel Varoujan prize in 1992 by the New England Poetry Club and was published in *Soho Square* (1991) · "That the Science of Cartography is Limited" appeared in *Poetry Review*, also in *New Poetry* (Bloodaxe) 1993 and was awarded the bronze medal in the publication of *Poetry Olympians* (1992). It also appeared in *Poetry Review*.

I would like to thank the Ingram Merrill Foundation whose grant covered the period in which this book was written.

Several people were helpful in reading these poems. I would like to thank Kevin Casey and Jody Allen-Randolph for their comments. Also, Alice Quinn, Jill Bialosky, and Michael Schmidt.

IN A TIME OF VIOLENCE

THE SINGERS
*for M.R.*


The women who were singers in the West
lived on an unforgiving coast.
I want to ask was there ever one
moment when all of it relented,
when rain and ocean and their own
sense of home were revealed to them
as one and the same?
                            After which
every day was still shaped by weather,
but every night their mouths filled with
Atlantic storms and clouded-over stars
and exhausted birds.
                            And only when the danger
was plain in the music could you know
their true measure of rejoicing in

finding a voice where they found a vision.

# I

# Writing
# in a
# Time of Violence

A SEQUENCE

As in a city where the evil are permitted to have
authority and the good are put out of the way,
so in the soul of man, as we maintain, the
imitative poet implants an evil constitution, for
he indulges the irrational nature which has no
discernment of greater or less.

PLATO, *The Republic*, X

. . . . . .

# I THAT THE SCIENCE OF CARTOGRAPHY IS LIMITED

—and not simply by the fact that this shading of
forest cannot show the fragrance of balsam,
the gloom of cypresses,
is what I wish to prove.

When you and I were first in love we drove
to the borders of Connacht
and entered a wood there.

Look down you said: this was once a famine road.

I looked down at ivy and the scutch grass
rough-cast stone had
disappeared into as you told me
in the second winter of their ordeal, in

1847, when the crop had failed twice,
Relief Committees gave
the starving Irish such roads to build.

Where they died, there the road ended

and ends still and when I take down
the map of this island, it is never so
I can say here is
the masterful, the apt rendering of

the spherical as flat, nor
an ingenious design which persuades a curve
into a plane,
but to tell myself again that

the line which says woodland and cries hunger
and gives out among sweet pine and cypress,
and finds no horizon

will not be there.

When the Peep-O-Day Boys were laying fires down in
the hayricks and seed-barns of a darkening Ireland,
the art of portrait-painting reached its height
across the water.
The fire caught.
The flames cracked and the light showed up the scaffold,
and the wind carried staves of a ballad:
The flesh-smell of hatred.
And she climbed the stairs. Nameless composite.
Anonymous beauty-bait for the painter.
Rustling gun-coloured silks.
To set a seal on Augustan London.
And sat down.
The easel waits for her
and the age is ready to resemble her and
the small breeze cannot touch that powdered hair.
That elegance.
But I smell fire.
From Antrim to the Boyne the sky is reddening as
the painter tints alizerine crimson with a mite of yellow
mixed once with white and finds out
how difficult it is to make the skin
blush outside the skin.
The flames have crossed the sea.
They are at the lintel. At the door.
At the canvas,
At her mouth.
And the curve and pout
of supple dancing and the couplet rhyming

and the pomander scenting death-rooms and
the cabinetmaker setting his veneers
in honest wood—they are kindling for the flames.
And the dictates of reason and the blended sensibility
of tact and proportion—yes
the eighteenth century ends here
as her hem scorches and the satin
decoration catches fire. She is burning down.
As a house might. As a candle will.
She is ash and tallow. It is over.

*The daffodils are out & how*
*you would love the harebells by*
*the Blackwater now.*
*But Etty, you are wise to stay away.*
*London may be dull in this season.*
*Meath is no better I assure you.*
*Your copper silk is sewn*
*& will be sent and I envy you.*
*Noone talks of anything but famine.*
*I go nowhere—*
*not from door to carriage—but a cloth*
*sprinkled with bay rum & rose attar*
*is pressed against my mouth.*
*Our picnics by the river—*
*remember that one with Major Harris?—*
*our outings to the opera*
*& our teas*
*are over now for the time being.*
*Shall I tell you what I saw on Friday,*
*driving with Mama? A woman lying*
*across the Kells Road with her baby—*
*in full view. We had to go*
*out of our way*
*to get home & we were late*
*& poor Mama was not herself all day.*

This is St. Louis. Where the rivers meet.
  The Illinois. The Mississippi. The Missouri.
The light is in its element of Autumn.
  Clear. With yellow Gingko leaves falling.
There is always a nightmare. Even in such light.

  The weather must be cold now in Dublin.
And when skies are clear, frosts come
  down on the mountains and the first
inklings of winter will be underfoot in
  the crisp iron of a fern at dawn.

I stand in a room in the Museum.
  In one glass case a plastic figure
represents a woman in a dress,
  with crepe sleeves and a satin apron.
And feet laced neatly into suede.

  She stands in a replica of a cabin
on a steamboat bound for New Orleans.
  The year is 1860. Nearly war.
A notice says no comforts were spared. The silk
  is French. The seamstresses are Irish.

I see them in the oil-lit parlours.
  I am in the gas-lit backrooms.
We make in the apron front and from
  the papery appearance and crushable
look of crepe, a sign. We are bent over

in a bad light. We are sewing a last
sight of shore. We are sewing coffin ships.
    And the salt of exile. And our own
death in it. For history's abandonment
    we are doing this. And this. And

this is a button hole. This is a stitch.
    Fury enters them as frost follows
every arabesque and curl of a fern: this is
    the nightmare. See how you perceive it.
We sleep the sleep of exhaustion.

    We dream a woman on a steamboat
parading in sunshine in a dress we know
    we made. She laughs off rumours of war.
She turns and traps light on the skirt.
    It is, for that moment, beautiful.

The wounds are terrible. The paint is old.
The cracks along the lips and on the cheeks
cannot be fixed. The cotton lawn is soiled.
The arms are ivory dissolved to wax.

Recall the Quadrille. Hum the waltz.
Promenade on the yachtclub terraces.
Put back the lamps in their copper holders.
The carriage wheels on the cobbled quays.

And re-create Easter in Dublin.
Booted officers. Their mistresses.
Sunlight crisscrossing College Green.
Steam hissing from the flanks of horses.

Here they are. Cradled and cleaned.
Held close in the arms of their owners.
Their cold hands clasped by warm hands,
Their faces memorized like perfect manners.

The altars are mannerly with linen.
The lilies are whiter than surplices.
The candles are burning and warning:
Rejoice, they whisper. After sacrifice.

Horse chestnuts hold up their candles.
The Green is vivid with parasols.
Sunlight is pastel and windless.
The bar of the Shelbourne is full.

Laughter and gossip on the terraces.
Rumour and alarm at the barracks.
The Empire is summoning its officers.
The carriages are turning: they are turning back.

Past children walking with governesses,
Looking down, cossetting their dolls,
then looking up as the carriage passes,
the shadow chilling them. Twilight falls.

It is twilight in the dolls' museum. Shadows
remain on the parchment-coloured waists,
are bruises on the stitched cotton clothes,
are hidden in the dimples on the wrists.

The eyes are wide. They cannot address
the helplessness which has lingered in
the airless peace of each glass case:
To have survived. To have been stronger than

a moment. To be the hostages ignorance
takes from time and ornament from destiny. Both.
To be the present of the past. To infer the difference
with a terrible stare. But not feel it. And not know it.

About holiday rooms there can be
a solid feel at first. Then, as you go upstairs,
the air gets
a dry rustle of excitement

the way a new dress comes out of tissue paper,
up and out of it, and
the girl watching this thinks:
*Where will I wear it? Who will kiss me in it?*

Peter
was the name on the cot.
The cot was made of the carefully bought
scarcities of the nineteen-forties:
Oak. Tersely planed and varnished.
Cast-steel hinges.

I stood where the roof sloped into
paper roses,
in a room where a child once went to sleep,
looking at blue, painted lettering:

as he slept
someone had found for him
five pieces of the alphabet which said
the mauve petals of his eyelids as they closed out
the scalded hallway moonlight made of the ocean at
the end of his road.

Someone knew
the importance of giving him a name.

For years I have known
how important it is
not to name
the coffins, the murdered in them,
the deaths in alleyways and on doorsteps—

in case they rise out of their names
and I recognize

the child who slept peacefully
and the girl who guessed at her future in
the dress as it came out of its box,
falling free in
kick pleats of silk.

And what comfort can there be
in knowing that
in a distant room
his sign is safe tonight
and reposes its modest blues in darkness?

Or that outside his window
the name-eating elements—the salt wind, the rain—
must find
headstones to feed their hunger?

In my last year in College
I set out
to write an essay on
the Art of Rhetoric. I had yet to find

the country already lost to me
in song and figure as I scribbled down
names for sweet euphony
and safe digression.

And when I came to the word *insinuate*
I saw that language could writhe and creep
and the lore of snakes
which I had learned as a child not to fear—
because the Saint had sent them out of Ireland—
came nearer.

*Chiasmus. Litotes. Periphrasis.* Old
indices and agents of persuasion. How
I remember them in that room where
a girl is writing at a desk with
dusk already in
the streets outside. I can see her. I could say to her—

we will live, we have lived
where language is concealed. Is perilous.
We will be—we have been—citizens
of its hiding place. But it is too late

to shut the book of satin phrases,
to refuse to enter
an evening bitter with peat smoke,
where newspaper sellers shout headlines
and friends call out their farewells in
a city of whispers
and interiors where

the dear vowels
*Irish Ireland ours* are
absorbed into Autumn air,
are out of earshot in the distances
we are stepping into where we never

imagine words such as *hate*
and *territory* and the like—unbanished still
as they always would be—wait
and are waiting under
beautiful speech. To strike.

*II*

# Legends

. . . . . .

# THIS MOMENT

A neighbourhood.
At dusk.

Things are getting ready
to happen
out of sight.

Stars and moths.
And rinds slanting around fruit.

But not yet.

One tree is black.
One window is yellow as butter.

A woman leans down to catch a child
who has run into her arms
this moment.

Stars rise.
Moths flutter.
Apples sweeten in the dark.

LOVE

Dark falls on this mid-western town
where we once lived when myths collided.
Dusk has hidden the bridge in the river
which slides and deepens
to become the water
the hero crossed on his way to hell.

Not far from here is our old apartment.
We had a kitchen and an Amish table.
We had a view. And we discovered there
love had the feather and muscle of wings
and had come to live with us,
a brother of fire and air.

We had two infant children one of whom
was touched by death in this town
and spared: and when the hero
was hailed by his comrades in hell
their mouths opened and their voices failed and
there is no knowing what they would have asked
about a life they had shared and lost.

I am your wife.
It was years ago.
Our child is healed. We love each other still.
Across our day-to-day and ordinary distances
we speak plainly. We hear each other clearly.

And yet I want to return to you
on the bridge of the Iowa river as you were,
with snow on the shoulders of your coat
and a car passing with its headlights on:

I see you as a hero in a text—
the image blazing and the edges gilded—
and I long to cry out the epic question
my dear companion:
Will we ever live so intensely again?
Will love come to us again and be
so formidable at rest it offered us ascension
even to look at him?

But the words are shadows and you cannot hear me.
You walk away and I cannot follow.

The only legend I have ever loved is
The story of a daughter lost in hell.
And found and rescued there.
Love and blackmail are the gist of it.
Ceres and Persephone the names.
And the best thing about the legend is
I can enter it anywhere. And have.
As a child in exile in
A city of fogs and strange consonants,
I read it first and at first I was
An exiled child in the crackling dusk of
The underworld, the stars blighted. Later
I walked out in a summer twilight
Searching for my daughter at bedtime.
When she came running I was ready
To make any bargain to keep her.
I carried her back past whitebeams.
And wasps and honey-scented buddleias.
But I was Ceres then and I knew
Winter was in store for every leaf
On every tree on that road.
Was inescapable for each one we passed.
And for me.
It is winter
And the stars are hidden.
I climb the stairs and stand where I can see
My child asleep beside her teen magazines,
Her can of Coke, her plate of uncut fruit.
The pomegranate! How did I forget it?
She could have come home and been safe

And ended the story and all
Our heartbroken searching but she reached
Out a hand and plucked a pomegranate.
She put out her hand and pulled down
The French sound for apple and
The noise of stone and the proof
That even in the place of death,
At the heart of legend, in the midst
Of rocks full of unshed tears
Ready to be diamonds by the time
The story was told, a child can be
Hungry. I could warn her. There is still a chance.
The rain is cold. The road is flint-coloured.
The suburb has cars and cable television.
The veiled stars are above ground.
It is another world. But what else
Can a mother give her daughter but such
Beautiful rifts in time?
If I defer the grief I will diminish the gift.
The legend must be hers as well as mine.
She will enter it. As I have.
She will wake up. She will hold
The papery, flushed skin in her hand.
And to her lips. I will say nothing.

MOTHS

Tonight the air smells of cut grass.
Apples rust on the branches. Already summer is
a place mislaid between expectation and memory.

This has been a summer of moths.
Their moment of truth comes well after dark.
Then they reveal themselves at our window—
ledges and sills as a pinpoint. A glimmer.

The books I look up about them are full of legends:
Ghost-swift moths with their dancing assemblies at dusk.
Their courtship swarms. How some kinds may steer by
    the moon.

The moon is up. The back windows are wide open.
Mid-July light fills the neighbourhood. I stand by the
    hedge.

Once again they are near the windowsill—
fluttering past the fuchsia and the lavender,
which is knee-high, and too blue to warn them

they will fall down without knowing how
or why what they steered by became, suddenly,
what they crackled and burned around. They will perish—

I am perishing—on the edge and at the threshold of
the moment all nature fears and tends toward:

The stealing of the light. Ingenious facsimile.

And the kitchen bulb which beckons them makes my child's shadow longer than my own.

## AT THE GLASS FACTORY
## IN CAVAN TOWN


Today it is a swan:
             The guide tells us
these are in demand.
             The glass is made

of red lead and potash
             and the smashed bits
of crystal sinews
             and decanter stoppers

crated over there—
             she points—and shattered
on the stone wheel
             rimmed with emery.

Aromas of stone and
             fire. Deranged singing
from the grindstone.
             And behind that

a mirror—my
             daughters' heads turned
away in it—garnering
             grindstone and fire.

The glass blower goes
             to the furnace.
He takes a pole
             from the earth's

core: the earth's core
          is remembered in
the molten globe at
          the end of it.

He shakes the pole
          carefully to and fro.
He blows once. Twice.
          His cheeks puff and

puff up: he is
          a cherub at the very
edge of a cornice with
          a mouthful of zephyrs—

sweet intrusions into
          leaves and lace hems.
And now he lays
          the rod on its spindle.

It is red. It is
          ruddy and cooler.
It is cool now
          and as clear as

the distances of this
          county with its drumlins,
its herons, its closed-
          in waterways on which

we saw this morning
          as we drove over
here, a mated pair
          of swans. Such

blind grace as they
          floated with told us
they did not know
          that every hour,

every day, and
          not far away from
there, they were
          entering the legend of

themselves. They gave no
          sign of it. But what
caught my eye, my
          attention, was the safety

they assumed as
          they sailed their own
images. Here, now—
          and knowing that

the mirror still holds
          my actual flesh—
I could say to them:
          reflection is the first

myth of loss. But
            they floated away and
away from me as if
            no one would ever blow

false airs on them,
            or try their sinews
in the fire, at
            the core, and they

took no care
            not to splinter, they
showed no fear
            they would end as

this one which is
            uncut yet still might:
a substance of its own
            future form, both

fraction and refraction
            in the deal-wood
crate at the door
            we will leave by.

# A SPARROW HAWK IN THE SUBURBS

At that time of year there is a turn in the road where
the hermit tones and meadow colours of
two seasons heal into
one another—

when the wild ladder of a winter scarf is stored away in
a drawer eased by candle-grease and lemon balm
is shaken out from
the linen press.

Those are afternoons when the Dublin hills are so close,
so mauve and blue, we can be certain dark
will bring rain and
it does to

the borrowed shears and the love-seat in the garden where
a sparrow hawk was seen through the opal-
white of apple trees
after Easter. And

I want to know how it happened that those days of
    bloom when
rumours of wings and sightings—always seen by
someone else, somewhere else—
filled the air,

together with a citrus drizzle of petals and clematis
    opening,
and shadows waiting on a gradual lengthening
in the light our children
stayed up

later by, over pages of wolves and dragons and learned to
measure the sanctuary of darkness by a small
danger—how and why
they have chilled

into these April nights I lie awake listening for wings I
    will
never see above the cold frames and
last frosts of our
back gardens.

Thinking of ageing on a summer day
  of rain and more rain
I took a book down from a shelf
   and stopped to read
and found myself—
  how did it happen?—
   reflecting on
the absurd creation of the water clock.
   Drops collected
on the bell-tongues of fuchsia
  outside my window.
    Apple-trees
  dripped. I read about
the clepsydra: invention of an ancient world,
  which reconciled
    element to argument
  before the alphabet
   had crossed the Hellespont:
   Water dripped
  from above
and turned a wheel
   which was about to turn
a dial when I looked up and saw
   the rain had stopped.
  *How could they have?* I thought.
   Taken an element, that is.
Which swallowed faces, stars, irises, Narcissus.
  And posed as frost, ice, snow.

And had a feel for
the theatre
and catastrophe of floods. And,
in an August storm,
could bring the moon to heel.
And reduced it
to this? And the sun came out and
the afternoon cleared.
And in half-an-hour—
maybe even less—
every trace of rain had disappeared.

# IN WHICH THE ANCIENT HISTORY
# I LEARN IS NOT MY OWN


The linen map
hung from the wall.
The linen was shiny
and cracked in places.
The cracks were darkened by grime.
It was fastened to the classroom wall with
a wooden batten on
a triangle of knotted cotton.

The colours
were faded out
so the red of Empire—
the stain of absolute possession—
the mark once made from Kashmir
to the oast-barns of the Kent
coast south of us was
underwater coral.

Ireland was far away
and farther away
every year.
I was nearly an English child.
I could list the English kings.
I could name the famous battles.
I was learning to recognize
God's grace in history.

And the waters
of the Irish sea,
their shallow weave
and cross-grained blue green
had drained away
to the pale gaze
of a doll's china eyes—
a stare without recognition or memory.

*We have no oracles,*
*no rocks or olive trees,*
*no sacred path to the temple*
*and no priestesses.*
The teacher's voice had a London accent.
This was London. 1952.
It was Ancient History Class.
She put the tip

of the wooden
pointer on the map.
She tapped over ridges and dried-
out rivers and cities buried in
the sea and seascapes which
had once been land.
And stopped.
*Remember this, children.*

*The Roman Empire was*
*the greatest Empire*
*ever known—*
*until our time of course—*
*while the Delphic Oracle*
*was reckoned to be*
*the exact centre*
*of the earth.*

Suddenly
I wanted
to stand in front of it.
I wanted to trace over
and over the weave of my own country.
To read out names
I was close to forgetting.
Wicklow. Kilruddery. Dublin.

To ask
where exactly
was my old house?
Its brass One and Seven.
Its flight of granite steps.
Its lilac tree whose scent
stayed under your fingernails
for days.

*For days—*
she was saying—*even months,*
*the ancients traveled*
*to the Oracle.*
*They brought sheep and killed them.*
*They brought questions about tillage and war.*
*They rarely left with more*
*than an ambiguous answer.*

# THE HUGUENOT GRAVEYARD AT
# THE HEART OF THE CITY

It is the immodesty we bring to these
names which have eased into ours, and
their graves in the alcove of twilight,
which shadows their exile:

There is a flattery in being a destination.
There is a vanity in being the last resort.
They fled the Edict of Nantes—
hiding their shadows on the roads from France—

and now under brambles and granite
faith lies low with the lives it
dispossessed, and the hands it emptied out,
and the sombre dances they were joined in.

The buses turn right at Stephen's Green.
Car exhaust and sirens fill the air. See
the planted wildness of their rest and
grant to them the least loves asks of

the living. Say: *they had another life once.*
And think of them as they first heard of us—
huddled around candles and words failing as
the stubbon tongue of the South put

*oo* and *an* to the sounds of Dublin,
and of their silver fingers at the windowsill
in the full moon as they leaned out
to breathe the sweet air of Nimes

for the last time, and the flame
burned down in a dawn agreed upon
for their heart-broken leave-taking. And
for their sakes, accept in that moment,

this city with its colours of sky and day—
and which is dear to us and particular—
was not a place to them: merely
the one witty step ahead of hate which

is all that they could keep. Or stay.

# THE PARCEL

There are dying arts and
one of them is
the way my mother used to make up a parcel.
Paper first. Mid-brown and coarse-grained as wood.
The worst sort for covering a Latin book neatly
or laying flat at Christmas on a pudding bowl.
It was a big cylinder. She snipped it open
and it unrolled quickly across the floor.
All business, all distance.
Then the scissors.
Not a glittering let-up but a dour
pair, black thumb-holes,
the shears themselves the colour of the rained-
on steps a man with a grindstone climbed up
in the season of lilac and snapdragon
and stood there arguing the rate for
sharpening the lawnmower and the garden pair
and this one. All-in.
The ball of twine was coarsely braided
and only a shade less yellow than
the flame she held under the blunt
end of the sealing wax until
it melted and spread into a brittle
terracotta medal.
Her hair dishevelled, her tongue between her teeth,
she wrote the address in the quarters
twine had divided the surface into.
Names and places. Crayon and fountain pen.
The town underlined once. The country twice.
It's ready for the post

she would say and if we want to know
where it went to—
a craft lost before we missed it—watch it go
into the burlap sack for collection.
See it disappear. Say
this is how it died
out: among doomed steamships and outdated trains,
the tracks for them disappearing before our eyes,
next to station names we can't remember
on a continent we no longer
recognize. The sealing wax cracking.
The twine unravelling. The destination illegible.

LAVA CAMEO
(A brooch carved on volcanic rock)


I like this story—

My grandfather was a sea captain.
My grandmother always met him when his ship docked.
She feared the women at the ports—

except that it is not a story,
more a rumour or a folk memory,
something thrown out once in a random conversation;
a hint merely.

If I say wool and lace for her skirt and
crepe for her blouse
in the neck of which is pinned a cameo,
carved out of black, volcanic rock;

if I make her pace the Cork docks, stopping
to take down her parasol as a gust catches
the silk tassels of it—

then consider this:

there is a way of making free with the past,
a pastiche of what is
real and what is
not, which can only be
justified if you think of it

not as sculpture but syntax:

a structure extrinsic to meaning which uncovers
the inner secret of it:

She will die at thirty-one in a fever ward.
He will drown nine years later in the Bay of Biscay.
They will never even be
sepia, and so I put down

the gangplank now between the ship and the ground.
In the story, late afternoon has become evening.
They kiss once, their hands touch briefly.
Please.

Look at me, I want to say to her: show me
the obduracy of an art which can
arrest a profile in the flux of hell.

Inscribe catastrophe.

THE SOURCE

The adults stood
making sounds of disappointment.

We were high up in the Wicklow hills,
in a circle of whins and lilacs.

We were looking for the source of a river.
We never found it.

Instead, we drove to its northern edge.
And there the river leaned into the afternoon—
all light, all intrusion—
the way a mirror interrupts a room.

See me kneeling in a room
whose boundary
is fog and the dusk of a strange city.

The mirror shows a child in bad light.

From the inlaid box I lift up something
closed in tissue paper.
My mother's hair. A whole coil of it.
It is the colour of corn harvested in darkness.

As the light goes,
I hold in my hand the coarse weight and
hopeless safe-keeping

and there comes back to me
the dialect of the not-found.

Maybe. Nearly. It could almost be.

## LEGENDS
*for Eavan Frances*


Tryers of firesides,
twilights. There are no tears in these.

Instead, they begin the world again,
making the mountain ridges blue
and the rivers clear and the hero fearless—

and the outcome always undecided
so the next teller can say *begin* and
*again* and astonish children.

Our children are our legends.
You are mine. You have my name.
My hair was once like yours.

And the world
is less bitter to me
because you will retell the story.

# Anna Liffey

. . . . . .

# ANNA LIFFEY

*Life,* the story goes,
Was the daughter of Cannan,
And came to the plain of Kildare.
She loved the flatlands and the ditches
And the unreachable horizon.
She asked that it be named for her.
The river took its name from the land.
The land took its name from a woman.

•

A woman in the doorway of a house.
A river in the city of her birth.

•

There, in the hills above my house,
The river Liffey rises, is a source.
It rises in rush and ling heather and
Black peat and bracken and strengthens
To claim the city it narrated.
Swans. Steep falls. Small towns.
The smudged air and bridges of Dublin.

•

Dusk is coming.
Rain is moving east from the hills.

If I could see myself
I would see
A woman in a doorway.
Wearing the colours that go with red hair.
Although my hair is no longer red.

.

I praise
The gifts of the river.
Its shiftless and glittering
Retelling of a city,
Its clarity as it flows,
In the company of runt flowers and herons,
Around a bend at Islandbridge
And under thirteen bridges to the sea.
Its patience at twilight—
Swans nesting by it,
Neon wincing into it.

.

Maker of
Places, remembrances,
Narrate such fragments for me:

One body. One spirit.
One place. One name.
The city where I was born.
The river that runs through it.
The nation which eludes me.

Fractions of a life
It has taken me a lifetime
To claim.

    •

I came here in a cold winter.

I had no children. No country.
I did not know the name for my own life.

My country took hold of me.
My children were born.

I walked out in a summer dusk
To call them in.

One name. Then the other one.
The beautiful vowels sounding out home.

    •

Make of a nation what you will
Make of the past
What you can—

There is now
A woman in a doorway.

It has taken me
All my strength to do this.

Becoming a figure in a poem.

Usurping a name and a theme.

　　　•

A river is not a woman.
　Although the names it finds,
　　The history it makes
And suffers—
　The Viking blades beside it,
　　The muskets of the Redcoats,
　　　the flames of the Four Courts
Blazing into it—
　Are a sign.
　　Anymore than
A woman is a river,
　Although the course it takes,
　　Through swans courting and distraught willows,
Its patience
　Which is also its powerlessness,
　　From Callary to Islandbridge,
　　And from source to mouth,
Is another one.
　　　　And in my late forties
Past believing
　　Love will heal
　　What language fails to know
And needs to say—
　What the body means—
　　I take this sign

•

And I make this mark:
    A woman in the doorway of her house.
    A river in the city of her birth.
The truth of a suffered life.
    The mouth of it.


    •


The seabirds come in from the coast.
The city wisdom is they bring rain.
I watch them from my doorway.
I see them as arguments of origin—
Leaving a harsh force on the horizon,
Only to find it
Slanting and falling elsewhere.

Which water—
The one they leave or the one they pronounce—
Remembers the other?

I am sure
The body of an ageing woman
Is a memory
And to find a language for it
Is as hard
As weeping and requiring
These birds to cry out as if they could
Recognize their element
Remembered and diminished in
A single tear.


    •

An ageing woman
Finds no shelter in language.
She finds instead
Single words she once loved
Such as "summer" and "yellow"
And "sexual" and "ready"
Have suddenly become dwellings
For someone else—
Rooms and a roof under which someone else
Is welcome, not her. Tell me,
Anna Liffey,
Spirit of water,
Spirit of place,
How is it on this
Rainy autumn night
As the Irish sea takes
The names you made, the names
You bestowed, and gives you back
Only wordlessness?

.

Autumn rain is
Scattering and dripping
From carports
And clipped hedges.
The gutters are full.

When I came here
I had neither
Children nor country.
The trees were arms.
The hills were dreams.

I was free
To imagine a spirit
In the blues and greens,
The hills and fogs
Of a small city.

My children were born.
My country took hold of me.
A vision in a brick house.
Is it only love
that makes a place?

I feel it change:
My children are
Growing up, getting older.
My country holds on
To its own pain.

I turn off
The harsh yellow
Porch light and
Stand in the hall.
Where is home now?

Follow the rain
Out to the Dublin hills.
Let it become the river.
Let the spirit of place be
A lost soul again.

.

In the end
It will not matter
That I was a woman. I am sure of it.
The body is a source. Nothing more.
There is a time for it. There is a certainty
About the way it seeks its own dissoloution.
Consider rivers.
They are always en route to
Their own nothingness. From the first moment
They are going home. And so
When language cannot do it for us,
Cannot make us know love will not diminish us,
There are these phrases
Of the ocean
To console us.
Particular and unafraid of their completion.
In the end
Everything that burdened and distinguished me
Will be lost in this:
I was a voice.

STORY

Two lovers in an Irish wood at dusk
are hiding from an old and vengeful king.

The wood is full of sycamore and elder.
And set in that nowhere which is anywhere:

And let the woman be slender. As I was at twenty.
And red-haired. As I was until recently.

They cling together listening to his hounds
get nearer in the twilight and the spring

thickets fill with the sound of danger.
Blossoms are the colour of blood and capture.

We can be safe, they say. We can start
a rumour in the wood to reach the king—

that she has lost her youth. That her mouth is
cold. That this woman is growing older.

They do not know. They have no idea
how much of this: the ocean-coloured peace

of the dusk, and the way legend stresses it,
depend on her to be young and beautiful.

They start the rumour in the last light.
But the light changes. The distance shudders.

And suddenly what is happening is not
what happens to the lovers in the wood

or an angry king and his frantic hounds—
and the tricks and kisses he has planned.

But what is whispering out of sycamores.
And over river-noise. And bypasses harebells

and blue air. And is overheard by the birds
which are the elements of logic in an early

spring. And is travelling to enter a suburb
at the foothills of the mountains in Dublin.

And a garden with jasmine and poplars. And
a table at which I am writing. I am writing

a woman out of legend. I am thinking
how new it is—this story. How hard it will be to tell.

The evening was the same as any other.
I came out and stood on the step.
The suburb was closed in the weather

of an early spring and the shallow tips
and washed-out yellows of narcissi
resisted dusk. And crocuses and snowdrops.

I stood there and felt the melancholy
of growing older in such a season,
when all I could be certain of was simply

in this time of fragrance and refrain,
whatever else might flower before the fruit,
and be renewed, I would not. Not again.

A car splashed by in the twilight.
Peat smoke stayed in the windless
air overhead and I might have missed it:

a presence. Suddenly. In the very place
where I would stand in other dusks, and look
to pick out my child from the distance,

was a shepherdess, her smile cracked,
her arm injured from the mantelpieces
and pastorals where she posed with her crook.

Then I turned and saw in the spaces
of the night sky constellations appear,
one by one, over roof-tops and houses,

and Cassiopeia trapped: stabbed where
her thigh met her groin and her hand
her glittering wrist, with the pin-point of a star.

And by the road where rain made standing
pools of water underneath cherry trees,
and blossoms swam on their images,

was a mermaid with invented tresses,
her breasts printed with the salt of it and all
the desolation of the North Sea in her face.

I went nearer. They were disappearing.
Dusk had turned to night but in the air—
did I imagine it?—a voice was saying:

*This is what language did to us. Here
is the wound, the silence, the wretchedness
of tides and hillsides and stars where*

*we languish in a grammar of sighs,
in the high-minded search for euphony,
in the midnight rhetoric of poesie.*

*We cannot sweat here. Our skin is icy.*
*We cannot breed here. Our wombs are empty.*
*Help us to escape youth and beauty.*

*Write us out of the poem. Make us human*
*in cadences of change and mortal pain*
*and words we can grow old and die in.*

## WE ARE THE ONLY ANIMALS
## WHO DO THIS

I saw a statue yesterday. A veiled woman.
Head and shoulders only. Up on a pedestal.
A veil of grief covering her whole face.
I stood there, caught by surprise, my
car keys getting warmer in one hand,
both of us women in our middle years,
but hers were fixed, set and finished in
a mutton-fat creaminess, a seamless flutter in
marble revealed by a sudden brightness
from the window behind me and other parts
were as dark as the shell of a swan mussel.

I saw my mother weep once. It was under
circumstances I can never, even now,
weave into or reveal by these cadences.
As I watched, and I was younger then,
I could see that weeping itself has no cadence.
It is unrhythmical, unpredictable and
the intake of breath one sob needs to
become another sob, so one tear can succeed
another, is unmusical: whoever the muse is
or was of weeping, she has put the sound of it
beyond the reach of metric-makers, music-makers.

I went up to her. At the well
of the throat where tears start,
there the artist must have started,
I was sure of it. From there upwards—
chin, lips, skin lines, eyelids—all
had been chiselled out with the veil in

the same, indivisible act of definition
which had silenced her. No sound. Not one.
No dissonance of grief in a small room on
a summer evening. Just a mineral grace
in which she had found a rhythm to weep by.

The rhythm of summer was unstoppable: a rapt
heat waited for the blackbird to say dusk
is coming, is about to be, will be able to
fold the ladysmock, cowslips and the grey
undertips of the mulberry leaves into that
translucence which is all darkness can be in
this season. The room was curtained, quiet.
We sat at right angles. I knew the late
sun would never make the cinnamon-and-
chintz pansies on those armrests grow
more or perish there. And my mother wept.

An object of the images we make is
what we are and how we lean out and
over the perfect surface where
our features in water greet and save us.
No weeping there: only the element
claiming its emblem. A last wheat-coloured
brightness filled the room. She dried her tears.
She put one hand up to her throat and pulled,
between her thumb and forefinger, the rope
of light there. "Did you know" she said
"some people say that pearls are tears?"

I could not ask her, she could not tell me
why something had once made her weep.
Had made her cover up her mouth and eyes
in the slow work of the moth fed on
white mulberry leaves. Had made her say:
from now on let daylight be black-
and-white and menial in-betweens and
let the distances be made of silk. My
distances were made of grit and the light
rain throws away in the hour between planets.
And rush-hour traffic. My keys were ready.

What she knew was gone and what I
wanted to know she had never known:
the moment her sorrow entered marble—
the exact angle of the cut at which
the sculptor made the medium remember
its own ordeal in the earth, the aeons
crushing and instructing it until it wept itself
into inches, atoms of change. Above all,
whether she flinched as the chisel found
that region her tears inferred,
where grief and its emblems are inseparable.

# A WOMAN PAINTED ON A LEAF

I found it among curios and silver.
in the pureness of wintry light.

A woman painted on a leaf.

Fine lines drawn on a veined surface
in a handmade frame.

This is not my face. Neither did I draw it.

A leaf falls in a garden.
The moon cools its aftermath of sap.
The pith of summer dries out in starlight.

A woman is inscribed there.

This is not death. It is the terrible
suspension of life.

I want a poem
I can grow old in. I want a poem I can die in.

I want to take
this dried-out face,
as you take a starling from behind iron,
and return it to its element of air, of ending—

so that autumn
which was once
the hard look of stars,
the frown on a gardener's face,
a gradual bronzing of the distance,

will be,
from now on,
a crisp tinder underfoot. Cheekbones. Eyes. Will be
a mouth crying out. Let me.

Let me die.